Created to Lead

A fresh perspective for women seeking God's path to their purpose and their highest potential

D1520273

Karen Zeigler

Copyright © 2014 by Karen Zeigler

All rights reserved. No portion of this book may be reproduced, stored in a retrieval system, or transmitted in any form or by any means—electronic, mechanical, photocopy, recording, scanning, or other—except for brief quotations in critical reviews or articles, without the prior written permission of the author.
ISBN: 1503059618
ISBN 13: 9781503059610

This book is dedicated to:

My family, who sacrificed time and income while I pursued my dream of writing and raising up women leaders: my husband, Dwayne Zeigler, and my daughter, Haley Swats.

The beautiful women leaders who helped develop the Personal Growth Map for women who desire to fulfill their call to lead: Angela Brizel, Kimberly Berger, Andrea Hollan, Rachel Cossette, Katie O'Bannon, Jennie Stovall, and Jen Diederich.

My prayer warriors, who lifted me up when I needed it most: Tamara Chilver, Morgan Hendrix, Crystal Miller, Gail Ross, Julie Shematz, Donlyn Turnbull, and Lisa Sadler.

My editor, Ginger Kolbaba, who stretched me as a writer and made this book one hundred times better than it was when originally drafted.

Contents

one

Cooking, Crafts & Condemnation

Good communication is just as stimulating as
black coffee, and just as hard to sleep after.
—Anne Morrow Lindbergh

It all started with four friends over coffee. You never know
what will happen when you get strong-minded Christian
women together who have a heart for serving God. While
at first it seemed like an ordinary gathering, we soon realized it was a divine appointment. We were all leaders of different women's small groups at our church: one led marrieds, two led singles of different ages, and one led a group
of diverse ages and backgrounds.

As we chatted about what was going on in our groups,
one leader asked, "What do women need?"

We each looked at one another with thoughtful
smiles—but no answers. Finally, we moved on to easier topics, like our families, our jobs, and the exciting things on
the horizon for each of us.

Afterward, I couldn't shake that question. I knew in
my heart, understanding the nature of our gender, that

the answer was not "Nothing." They've written film scripts about what women need without encompassing it all, so *nothing* certainly wasn't the answer!

As I left the coffee shop that day, I reflected on my experience of discovering what I, as a woman, needed—and in particular with figuring out my purpose. Often we rely on the church to help us discover it. I thought church should be an encouraging and helpful place to realize and fulfill a person's purpose, yet from my own experience and knowing the experience of others, often the church provides the most obstacles to it. At least that was the case for me.

I thought back to my first experience going to my church's women's ministry—surely a place that would help me discover and grow fully into the woman I was created and called to be. A woman in a floral dress with a doily collar stood at the door waiting to greet everyone with, "Welcome to women's ministry—a place where you'll find cooking, crafts, and condemnation."

Well, of course she didn't say that, but she may as well have. In the late 1980s, there seemed to be only two kinds of women in church: those who stayed at home and those who "had to work" (note the condemnation). I was neither. I graduated college with a finance degree and I chose to have a career.

I had tried cooking. I wasn't good at it. I burnt toast and made crunchy spaghetti. I served fried chicken that was raw in the middle. And more important, I just didn't enjoy it.

As for crafts, while I didn't loathe crafts as much as cooking, I saw them as somewhat of a leisure sport. As a career woman, my days and even some evenings were filled with work. Any spare moment was filled with family—no spare time for crafts.

So after my initial experience, I quickly dismissed the need for women's ministry. It didn't fill the void of finding and fulfilling God's purpose for my life or how I was to balance it all and keep my sanity.

Six years later, after the birth of my daughter, I decided to give women's ministry another try. I thought surely, as a mother, I would have a common bond with the other women—and this time I would find what I needed; I would find my place and purpose. Instead I discovered that not much had changed. While my choice of career as a married woman had been excused as lunacy—or at least, that's how I felt they looked at it—being a mother and continuing a career was now a downright sin. What kind of woman would call herself a Christian yet forsake her family? Feeling judged and rejected, I again wrote off women's ministry for the most part. It seemed that if my natural bent were toward more domestic endeavors, I would have a great training ground. But if I chose a different path; I was on my own.

I knew I was called to be a leader. I had that clear skill set. But I also understood that *every Christian* is called to lead—whether we work outside the home or work inside the home raising a family. One option doesn't make our leadership calling null and void. Nor does our gender cancel our calling to influence others.

I yearned for the church to help me. I desperately wanted them to provide the tools I needed to develop my leadership skills and grow them. Yet the only talk of leadership in those circles focused on "male responsibilities." And because I wasn't necessarily hardwired to fit neatly in the domestic category, I felt as though the women at my church weren't sure how to deal with me. Nor I with them.

Women Trailblazers in the Church

For me, the only redeeming grace in women's ministry was the great Bible studies. The likes of Beth Moore, Joyce Meyer, and others had come on the scene, and I, along with other women, loved studying my Bible. While the primary objectives of attending a women's Bible study were a thirst for Bible knowledge, a deeper relationship with God, and to connect with other women, I knew there was more to the phenomenon. I mean truthfully, we already had pastors and other great men who were teaching us the truth of God's Word. We could read and study the Bible as deep as we wanted to go. It wasn't the void of biblical truth or a means to study that had attracted us to these women.

These women were trailblazers! They were attempting things women had been discouraged and disqualified from for centuries. Greater than being trailblazers, they had accomplished things that I had longed for—that I believe every woman longs for. Despite their painful pasts, their hurts, and struggles, these Bible study leaders had discovered God's purpose for their lives and were leading strong.

How did these women go against stereotype to become the women God called them to be? I wondered. How did they discover their strengths and giftings?

While I admired these trailblazers and my knowledge of the Bible grew, women's ministry still left a gaping hole when it came to discovering my own purpose and to guide me in God's path for my life. And I realized that if I felt this way, many other women must also feel this way.

Fortunately my career in the financial industry put me on the path of personal growth, and leadership giants like Zig Ziglar, John Maxwell, and others were there to pave the way. I can remember walking out of my first Zig Ziglar conference with a bag full of books and tapes. From there it was a bunny trail of conferences, resources, and workshops that God divinely guided me through. Where women's ministry failed, strong Christian leaders outside the church guided me into finding where I best fit in and how best to use my talents.

While all this may seem like church bashing, I can say that my heart is truly on the opposite end of the spectrum. I have been in and involved in church since the day I was saved at age ten. Even during the busiest seasons of my life, when my daughter was young, our family rarely missed a Sunday. I love church, and many of the friends I have made there through the years are closer than family. I tell this story, even write this book, because my desire is for the church not to stop moving people toward salvation and their eternal reward in heaven but also to continue guiding women to find and fulfill God's purpose for them on earth. While I did not rest until I found the resources outside of the church to help me, I never waivered in my dedication to and love of the church.

Unfortunately, many women are vanishing from our churches. Could it be that women are leaving because they too haven't been able to find and fulfill their purpose there? And I can't think of a greater or faster way to accomplish finding purpose than through the local church.

We're All Called to Lead

As I grew more confident in my leadership abilities and learned more about how God uniquely gifted me, I began to realize that my being a woman *and* a leader wasn't a mistake. God didn't allow an *oopsy* in my life. He created me this way *on* purpose and *for* a purpose. And what was more exciting was that as I spent more time studying Scripture, I learned that God created and calls *all* Christian women to be leaders.

I know for some women that's difficult to grasp—especially since many of us have been told that men are called to be the leader in our homes and beyond. While I will leave that debate for the theologians and great writers on the subject, like Loren Cunningham and Jay Lee Grady (both men, by the way), I can say with certainty that the great commission applies to all believers (including women). It reads as follows:

> Go and make disciples of all nations, baptizing them in the name of the Father and of the Son and of the Holy Spirit, and teaching them to obey everything I have commanded you. And surely I am with you always, to the very end of the age. (Mt 28:19–20)

While Christ is the ultimate leader, people will not follow us to Him unless we first *lead them*. And creating disciples is all about teaching—a key leadership trait that all believers are called to possess (we'll expand on this trait in a few more pages). Further evidence of the call to leadership for all believers (not just men) manifests in two obvious ways. The first being the definition of the two words:

- *Christian*: an individual set apart (Lv 20:26) to lead others to Christ and teach them how to become His disciples (Mt 28:19–20).

- *Leader*: setting yourself apart from others and setting an example. In the *Business News Daily* article "How to Become a Great Leader," Michael Flanigan, vice president at Expressionary, sums up being a leader as follows: "It's not about being in charge or power, but rather caring for others and helping them achieve a common goal."

Our call to leadership is not about a position. Our call is about influence. To quote John Maxwell, "Leadership is influence." Christ was most notably the most influential leader of all time. Yet Christ never held a position. Instead His interest was always in seeking God and living a life of leadership. Christ doesn't care what our position is. We don't have to be a leader of a corporation or of a nonprofit or hold any position of leadership. We can be a stay-at-home mom, an administrative assistant, or a salesperson. Leadership is never about the job we do; it's about who we are and how we live.

And just in case carrying the leadership responsibility of the great commission isn't convincing enough, here are six additional passages that show us God's leadership call on our lives.

1. **Women were *created* to lead.**

> God blessed them and said, "Be fruitful and multiply. Fill the earth and *govern it.* Reign over the fish in the sea, the birds in the sky, and all the animals that scurry along the ground." (Gn 1:28 NLT; italics added)

God did not say, "Women, you be fruitful, and men, you govern the world." It takes both men and women to be fruitful and it takes men *and* women to govern the world that God has placed in our charge.

2. **Women are *commanded* to put on the character traits of a leader.**

Since you have been raised to new life with Christ, set your sights on the realities of heaven, where Christ sits in the place of honor at God's right hand. Think about the things of heaven, not the things of earth. For you died to this life, and your real life is hidden with Christ in God. And when Christ, who is your life, is revealed to the whole world, you will share in all his glory.

So put to death the sinful, earthly things lurking within you. Have nothing to do with sexual immorality, impurity, lust, and evil desires. Don't be greedy, for a greedy person is an idolater, worshiping the things of this world…Now is the time to get rid of anger, rage, malicious behavior, slander, and dirty language. Don't lie to each other, for you have stripped off your old sinful nature and all its wicked deeds. Put on your new nature, and be renewed as you learn to know your Creator and become like him. In this new life, it doesn't matter if you are a Jew or a Gentile, circumcised or uncircumcised, barbaric, uncivilized, slave, or free. Christ is all that matters, and he lives in all of us.

Since God chose you to be the holy people he loves, you must clothe yourselves with tenderhearted mercy, kindness, humility, gentleness, and patience. Make allowance for each other's faults, and forgive anyone who offends you. Remember, the Lord forgave you, so you must forgive others. Above all, clothe yourselves with love, which binds us all together in perfect harmony. And let the peace that comes from Christ rule in your hearts. For as members of one body you are called to live in peace. And always be thankful.

Let the message about Christ, in all its richness, fill your lives. Teach and counsel each other with all the wisdom he gives. Sing psalms and hymns and spiritual songs to God with thankful hearts. And whatever you do or say, do it as a representative of the Lord Jesus, giving thanks through him to God the Father. (Col 3:1–5, 8–17 NLT)

While this is a long passage, it lays out the character traits every Christian—including women—is to put on. Honesty, humility, and many others. You'll find these same character traits in any secular book on leadership that you pick up.

3. Women are *called* to the highest title of leadership: Ambassador.

We are Christ's ambassadors, God making His appeal as it were through us. We [as Christ's personal representatives] beg you for His sake to lay hold of the divine favor [now offered you] *and* be reconciled to God. (2 Cor 5:20 AMP)

The definition of ambassador is a diplomatic official of the highest rank, sent by one sovereign or state to another as its resident representative. So not only have you been called to be a leader, but you have also been given the highest rank of leadership possible.

4. Women were given a vision to *cast*.

The fruit of the Spirit is love, joy, peace, patience, kindness, goodness, faithfulness, gentleness, self-control; against such things there is no law. (Gal 5:22–23 NASB)

One of the primary jobs of a leader is to cast the vision of the organization (or tribe of people) she leads. As Christian leaders, we are called to cast the vision for what life with Christ looks like. When our lives look like that, we attract people. That's what leaders do.

5. Women are commanded to *communicate* a greater purpose.

Each of you should use whatever gift you have received to serve others, as faithful stewards of God's grace in its various forms. (1 Pt 4:10 NIV)

Stewards in this context refers to managers, and management is a form of leadership. When we manage the gifts we've been given for a greater purpose, our lives are attractive to others. And attracting people is what leaders do.

6. Women are called to build *community*.

The human body has many parts, but the many parts make up one whole body. So it is with the body of Christ. Some of us are Jews, some are Gentiles, some are slaves, and some are free. But we have all been baptized into one body by one Spirit, and we all share the same Spirit.

Yes, the body has many different parts, not just one part. If the foot says, "I am not a part of the body because I am not a hand," that does not make it any less a part of the body. And if the ear says, "I am not part of the body because I am not an eye," would that make it any less a part of the body? If the whole body were an eye, how would you hear? Or if your whole body were an ear, how would you smell anything?

But our bodies have many parts, and God has put each part just where he wants it. How strange a body would be if it had only one part! Yes, there are many parts, but only one body. The eye can never say to the hand, "I don't need you." The head can't say to the feet, "I don't need you."

In fact, some parts of the body that seem weakest and least important are actually the most necessary. And the parts we regard as less honorable are those we clothe with the greatest care. So we carefully protect those parts that should not be seen, while the more honorable parts do not require this special care. So God has put the body together such that extra honor and care are given to those parts that have less dignity. This makes for harmony among the members, so that all the members care for each other. If one part suffers, all the parts suffer with it, and if one part is honored, all the parts are glad. All of you together are Christ's body, and each of you is a part of it. (1 Cor 12:12–27 NLT)

Leaders understand that everyone on the team plays an important role. There are no unimportant roles. It takes everyone to get the job done. Christians also are given that same instruction in the passage above where it talks about the different parts of the body, their function, and how God ordained each one for a purpose.

You (my fellow Christian woman) and I have been called to lead. Scripture offers no excuses! God is clear that the highest potential that He has for you is to lead. How we reach our great potential and discover our purpose is what this book is about.

There Has to Be an Answer!
As I left the coffee time with my leader friends, I continued to dwell on my own experience and the simple, but so complex, question of what women need. Sadly, this desire to discover our life's purpose still exists for many women today. I know—I coach them every day. And much like my own experience, women are unable to discover their purpose at church either.

As that day turned to weeks, I couldn't get the question out of my head: What do women need? It was that question that drove me to weeks of prayer. One day I was repeating the question over and over while I was in the shower: "What do women need? What do women need? What do women need?" (I didn't even consider that I was praying; I was just talking to myself as usual.)

I guess there is something to the cliché, "Cleanliness is next to godliness," because God decided to interrupt the conversation I was having with myself. In my spirit I heard,

Get over it…
Get it together…
Get on with it!

God's Answer to My Prayer
I pondered and prayed about what that meant for the entire day. I knew the work God had done in my life. I knew the

steps I had taken to move beyond my past, my hurts, my struggles (some intentional, some God ordained) to understand who I was in Christ, how He had created me, and what the purpose in my life was. As I lay down to sleep that night (don't you love how God won't let you sleep when He's up to something?), the process of that discovery flooded my mind like words being written feverishly on a chalkboard: I had figured out the answer to the question. And I knew the solution: a new women's Personal Growth Map.

Excitedly the next morning, I shared the women's Personal Growth Map with my friends from the coffee shop. They were pumped about the possibility of the map and the impact it could have on changing women's lives. The coffee shop foursome turned into a self-made committee. In addition, we added a few young twentysomething leaders to round out the input from the various women's demographics. As a group we began to meet monthly to dig deeper into what the issues were that women needed to Get Over, Get Together, and Get On With. We defined the goals of each of those phases. We researched the available resources. Out of all our hard work and effort, we developed a map for personal growth for women. A map that provides a guide to help women find healing and wholeness to overcome the pains of life. A map that will guide them to maintain balance, discover their purpose, and strengthen them in mind, body, and spirit. A map that encourages women to fulfill their purpose and lead strong by serving others with their strengths and talents. This map, infused with grace and motivation, became

Moving On...

Moving Up...

Moving Out!

The old model of developing a woman was about "doing": cooking, crafts, and the many actions of being a wife and mother. The new Personal Growth Map for women is about "being." Being the woman God uniquely created you to be. More important, it is about becoming the *leader* Christ has called you to be. Call it what you will—influencer, for instance—but you *are* a leader. You may be leading a room full of precious, sticky little faces or the financial oversight committee for a large corporation. But you're a leader. And a vital one at that! While most women see leadership as a position and thus don't see themselves as leaders, the truth is that leadership is about influence. God has uniquely created women with the gift of influence.

Being a Christian woman is not about what you do but about who you are. Discovering who you are and your unique call to leadership involves getting clear of the past, getting a handle on the areas of life that tend to slow you down, understanding how you were created, grabbing hold of your purpose, and seeing the vision God has cast for your future. And most important, it's about helping you set out with a determined action toward that destination.

But before we jump into the map for growing women into godly leaders, I want to share more of my story. I believe it will save you a few decades on your leadership journey and help you see more clearly the connection I was missing up until the time God spoke those three phrases to me: Get over it, get it together, and get on with it.

two

The Why behind the What

I think we all wish we could erase some dark times in our lives. But all of life's experiences, bad and good, make you who you are. Erasing any of life's experiences would be a great mistake.
—Luis Miguel, *award-winning singer*

Think back to a childhood experience you have observed—with your own child or someone else's—in which a toddler was going through separation anxiety. Mom left the room and the toddler cried for what seemed like hours. Whether tired, hungry, or scared, this little one would run to Mommy for comfort and protection.

Mom represents life, comfort, protection, love, and so much more. The child separated from his mother during this stage usually suffers from what psychologists label *attachment disorder*. The resulting anxiety, anger, distrust, addictions, impulsiveness, and lack of emotion are often the great makings of Hollywood psycho movies like *Fatal Attraction* or *Orphan*.

I was that child. Thank God for His grace I am not that adult. I lost my mother when I was a toddler, at the height of that clingy stage.

Unfortunately, the tragedy didn't end there. At the time of my mother's death, my father had just returned home on honorable discharge from the Vietnam War. His discharge was due to manic-depressive schizophrenia. Talk about adding insult to injury. The courts (because my parents didn't have a will) deemed my father an unfit parent—as they should have—and gave custody to my maternal grandparents.

Unfortunately, my grandparents weren't the sweet little old people (like you see on TV) who spend time with their grandkids baking cookies or taking them fishing. Instead, my grandfather was a lifelong alcoholic, and my grandmother was a mean and bitter woman—I suppose from having raised five kids in those conditions. I'm sure her life up to that point had been hard. Her last child was almost out of the house, and she was probably ready to take a much-needed reprieve when she was thrust into caring for a toddler going through detachment from her mother and who (according to her) cried inconsolably for weeks.

I never discovered what made my grandmother so bitter—was it the years of living with an alcoholic, the death of a daughter, or being saddled with a toddler with little means to provide support for everything a small child needed? All I could understand at the time was that I was the brunt of her mental and emotional abuse. For instance, I remember one Christmas I got coal and switches, because according to her, I had been a bad child that year.

While oftentimes adopted children can experience reattachment with their new parent, I never did. I can recall only a handful of times when I experienced the motherly touch of love as she stroked my hair as I laid my head in her lap on the front-porch swing. Isolated and lonely, as she rarely would let me go anywhere, I don't remember experiencing it elsewhere either.

In third grade my life took a turn for the worse. We were out for a drive with my grandfather, who was drunk (Grandma—poor and from a different era—had never gotten her license), when we came face-to-face with a wide concrete light pole. By God's grace, my grandmother snatched the wheel, and our lives were spared. However, the shock of that moment when we stared death in the face at the concrete pole seemed to jar in her a courage that she hadn't had before. In that moment she decided to leave my grandfather. Homeless, without transportation, and with only a social security check for an income, we were left with only one solution: to move in with her mother—my great-grandmother. If one grumpy grandmother wasn't enough to drive an adolescent insane, try two!

While an alcoholic father (in this case, my grandfather) may not be the best male role model, he *had* provided a male presence in my life up to that point. Even a poor presence provided protection—which was better than no presence. His absence left me extremely vulnerable. Shortly after moving into my great-grandmother's home, I discovered another round of pain and despair: my great-uncle would visit two to three times a year and sexually molest me.

Sexual abuse is devastating enough if it only occurs once, yet somehow I felt fortunate that mine was limited to only a few times a year when he visited. Somehow it made it seem better that at least it wasn't happening every week.

Still, even with that warped rationale, to a young girl who already felt worthless and abandoned, this pain seemed unbearable.

I had always shared a room with my grandmother, which I'm sure was another way God protected me. As I got older, I begged to have a room of my own. The only room that would work was a sleeping porch. If you've never been in an old plantation-style home, it's the equivalent of having a bed on your lanai. While I couldn't sleep there in the winter, I pled to spend my summers in my own "room." My great-uncle happened to be visiting during one of my begging rants and convinced Grandmother that I was mature enough to sleep alone on the sleeping porch. Little did I know the plans he had. I was just thrilled that he'd taken my side and convinced Grandmother that I should be on my own.

On my first night in my new room, he decided to pay me a visit. The molestation seemed to be taking a turn for the worse as he started to crawl into the bed. I screamed bloody murder, which sent him running back to the door from which he had entered. Within a few seconds, my grandmother, my molesting uncle, and his wife were all standing in my doorway, wondering what had happened. After that incident, the next morning, I summoned the courage to tell my grandmother what my great-uncle had done. Though I'm not sure I realized it then, I'm certain he would have raped me that night if I had not screamed for help.

Instead of listening and acting on my confession, my grandmother dismissed it, called it nonsense, and insisted I not tell anyone. I felt crushed. The only two people I felt I could trust at all were another uncle and an aunt (my mom's siblings), yet out of shame, I never told them. They lived a couple hundred miles away in opposite directions, busy with their adult lives and families. A week or two of summer vacation at their respective houses was all I was able to use to get away from the hopeless situation that was home. So for most of the year, I suffered—isolated and alone.

My Life-changing Moment

We lived in a little town of less than six hundred people. The town had two churches—one Baptist and one Methodist. The Baptist church was a block from my home, and with no transportation or religious background in my family, that became the church of choice because I could walk there. Though my grandmothers never went, they were happy to get rid of a pesky kid once or twice a week for a couple of hours. It was there on a Sunday morning not long after I started attending that from the back row, I gave my life to Christ. I still remember what the pastor said that day: "We are all unworthy, except by the shed blood of Jesus Christ." When I heard those words, my heart leapt to know that I was not alone in my feelings of unworthiness, and better yet, with Jesus, I didn't need to feel unworthy at all anymore. His love and death on the cross for me had made me worthy in God's eyes.

While I had walked into that little country church downtrodden, dejected, and ashamed, I walked out with a new hope of who I was in Christ. I was ten years old.

Although I accepted Jesus and my heart changed, little changed in my outward circumstances. My grandmother was still mean, and my uncle still visited his usual two to three times a year. While I was getting wiser to his schemes to molest me, it still happened on occasion. Feeling full of shame and more rejection from my grandmother's response, I never confided in anyone else about what was happening with my uncle or at home.

The only change that really occurred after I accepted Christ was that I began praying and reading my Bible. Proverbs was about all I could understand at that age, so I read that and the Psalms regularly. I wasn't sure what good it would do, but the pastor and youth leaders said it would help.

A Darker Pain

In spite of my church attendance, Bible reading, and prayer, by the time I was thirteen, I became deeply depressed. It could have been the cumulative effect of the abuse, the onset of preteen hormones, a direct attack by the enemy, or any number of things, but my thoughts turned to running away. And if not running away, suicide. The little town we lived in was more than twenty miles from any type of city, and I knew I would likely not get more than a couple of blocks from home before someone would pick me up and take me back. So I reasoned my way out of that option. While sometimes I considered suicide, I really didn't dwell there. Through the sermons I heard and the Scriptures I read, I knew God had an abundant life for me. I didn't necessarily want to end my life, I just wanted to end the misery of my life as it existed right then. I think even at that young age, the problem solver in my personality was hard at work trying to find a way to this better life God had promised. If it wasn't running away and it wasn't suicide, then the only happiness I could find was in the summer trips to my aunt and uncle's houses. So I reasoned perhaps one of them would let me live with them. I asked if they would let me move in. I'm sure if they had known more of the circumstances, they would have thought differently. But as it stood, they thought disrupting my home and school was not in my best interest.

The answer was no. My uncle was newly married, and my aunt had three kids she was raising. Unfortunately, their unintentional rejection continued to pile on the lies that the enemy was always throwing my way: *You're worthless. No one loves you. No one cares for you. No one wants you.*

An Unlikely Miracle

In the midst of my torment, God delivered an unlikely miracle. A few months prior to turning fourteen, God sent me an angel in the form of a young man named Dwayne. I still call him my Dw-angel today. We met in band camp a few weeks before I started high school.

As one of the new freshman girls, I seemed to garner the attention of three upperclassmen in particular. Dwayne, a junior, stood out above everyone. I was a quiet introvert; he was a gregarious extrovert. He was charming and so funny, and his Christian faith was evident in our conversations. As we became friends, my thoughts of running away or suicide slowly began to fade. I went from rejected and abused to accepted, loved, and adored. I went from depressed to giddy in puppy love. While the misery with my grandmothers didn't stop, I was distracted and crazy in love. And with a man (even though young at the time) on the scene, occupying every free moment and being the only thing I could talk about, the opportunities for abuse seemed to disappear. I continued to share a room with my grandmother, and most days I was out of the house hanging out with Dwayne or visiting his family.

While I'm not sure if his age slowed down his number of visits to south Georgia or that my grandmother may have questioned him in private, my great-uncle never again attempted to abuse me. It didn't matter, really; God had answered my prayer, and the abuse stopped.

So in love and ready to be rescued from the darkness that I was under, when I turned seventeen and within weeks of graduating high school, I married my Dw-angel and high school sweetheart. Many people tried to talk us out of marriage since we were so young—or they assumed I was pregnant and we "had" to marry (which wasn't the case)—but we both knew God had given us each other to love and cherish. While marriage is never without difficulty, I can truly say I love him as much today as I did those thirty-one years ago. He is a gift from God. He is a funny, loving, and gracious man of God. And boy, have I given him years of opportunity to exercise that grace with all the baggage that I brought into the relationship.

A Decades-Later Discovery
A few years ago (now in my forties), I crossed paths with the founder of Beauty from Ashes, a sex trafficking and sexual abuse ministry.

It was my horses and the founder's love of riding that brought us together. My life was full with family, youth ministry, church work, and volunteering with my husband with Fellowship of Christian Athletes. Even though having been sexually abused allowed me to empathize with the victims she ministers to, I really didn't have time to be part of her ministry. We became good horse-riding buddies, though, and after about three months, she invited me to her national training event for individuals serving or looking to establish similar ministries. It was a three-day event, and while I couldn't commit to all three days, I decided as a friend to show support by dropping in for a few hours to learn a bit more about what she did.

During the time I was there, she shared the statistics of women who end up prostituting or being sex trafficked. According to research, approximately 95 percent of women end up that way because they were abused as children. In fact, I was shocked to find out that it is a documented fact that between the ages of ten and thirteen, sexually abused children often run away from home. While the children believe they are running away from the terrible circumstances of their abuse to a better place, in an overwhelming number of cases, the result is them being picked up by abusers and traffickers for a life of sexual slavery and drug addiction.

As I listened to my friend speak about the harsh realities facing sexual abuse victims, I realized that God's hand was on my life! Even then, when I was in the deepest pit of despair and agony, He was there. He had spared my life from that tragedy for His greater purpose. But more so, through years of counseling, Bible study, and personal growth pursuits, He had redeemed the childhood pain, neglect, and abuse so that I could minister to women experiencing similar feelings of unworthiness, rejection, and being unloved.

Problems, People, and Pleasing God

So how does a young woman go from the verge of insanity to a happily married wife, mother, and respected leader?

It's not easy, as I'm sure you can imagine, but my personality played a big part of setting me out on the journey. By nature I am a problem solver (and boy did I have a lot of problems that needed solving!), and I have an intense desire to learn. The journey started with a deep yearning to experience the abundant life that I read about in Scripture and probably an equally burning desire not to repeat my family history of alcoholism, codependence, and mental instability.

After I graduated and settled into married life, my focus turned to earning a degree in finance, which I felt would equip me to break the chains of poverty. But I also felt as though God was calling me to something more. When I attended my church's women's ministry, thinking they would help me identify and grow that call, I was disappointed to learn they weren't equipped or interested in helping me grow in ways that, I felt, were beyond becoming an excellent homemaker. Ironically feeling outcast from my church's women's ministry because I wasn't a stay-at-home wife and mom sent me on a quest, primarily outside the church. While I thoroughly enjoyed studying Scripture through the Beth Moore studies and other studies, and I am confident God's Word transformed my life through them, I still held a lot of unanswered questions. A lot of problems left unsolved.

Fortunately for me, my first job out of college as a bank branch manager included lots of opportunities to study personal growth and leadership from top leaders—both Christian and secular. It was this environment of needing to get along with people, manage them, and motivate them to perform that was so challenging and full of problems. How could I manage them when I couldn't manage myself?

How could I communicate effectively when I knew only how to clam up and retreat? How could I teach others to be confident in their jobs when I wasn't even confident in my own skin? While the issues are far too many to count, that was how the journey started. In an effort to summarize what drove me to the solutions, my quest to grow into the leader I wanted to be boiled down to three things: problems, people, and pleasing God.

Problems were many: negative thoughts, emotional instability, lack of boundaries, low self-esteem, anger, and depression. I wanted healing, and by facing these myriad of problems through Bible study, reading books, and months of counseling, I was able to move on and find healing and wholeness. Understanding who I was (namely, that I wasn't what had happened to me), and more importantly, who I was in Christ, propelled me forward. Although it took much of my early twenties, it was freeing to move on from the past pains and hurts.

I then turned my attention to moving up by getting my life together in areas that can easily get out of whack for a busy wife, mother, and career woman. Earning a finance degree might seem like enough, but there is so much more to stewardship than understanding the numbers—such as living within your means, spending money wisely, giving, and saving for the future. In addition, there was self-care, time management, and much more I needed to learn. While life is never perfect, we certainly will find it difficult to grow deeper in our faith, understand our strengths and talents, and discover God's purpose for our lives when chaos reigns over our schedules and relationships.

Growing up with such dysfunction, it's easy to have a victim mindset that other people are the problem. Yet as I began to unearth all my problems, I quickly began to realize that people *weren't* the problem. I was! How they communicated with me, treated me, or dismissed me wasn't as much their doing as it was mine. My marriage didn't just depend on my husband communicating well but also on *my* communication. My ability to work in teams was as much my responsibility as it was the others on the team. My ability to manage well depended more than just the ability to fire those who got out of line but also to motivate and train those who desired to be part of the team. And even the times when I thought I could blame people for mistreating me, I learned those were my issues as well. I needed well-established boundaries about what was acceptable behavior and what wasn't. While the problems were all mine, adding people to the mix just magnified them. I couldn't control other people or their problems, but I could learn to control myself and minimize my problems.

If solving problems and getting along well with people wasn't incentive enough to pursue personal growth, then for me the ultimate goal was pleasing God. Emotional instability, anger, mistreating or disrespecting others, and mismanaging time and money were not only disruptive to my life but also displeasing to God. How could anyone see the peace, patience, kindness, goodness, and the other fruits of the Spirit in my life with all the baggage life circumstances had stacked in the way? Ultimately my journey wasn't just about solving my own problems or getting along better with people; it was about living a life that pleased God.

Crazy, Wonderful Journey to the Answer

It was this tragic, crazy, and wonderful journey that God used to equip me to answer this question: What do women need, and *why* do they need it? In a less-than-organized fashion, I had

- *gotten over* my past through counseling, reading books, and attending personal growth and leadership conferences and Bible study groups
- *gotten my life together* through studying finance, reading books on time management and purpose, and going to school to be a life coach
- *gotten on* with my purpose with much prayer and pursuit of my passions and giftings

As I healed, grew, and discovered God's plan for me, I grew in my desire to help others discover their own healing, growth, and purposes.

While the hurts and pains of your life may look different from mine, they still exist. The enemy has made sure to leave us with holes in our soul, which only God can heal and make whole again. God has done amazing things in your life: He knit you together in your mother's womb (Ps 139:13), promises to guide you along the best path for your life (Ps 32:8), and has a great plan to prosper you and give you hope (Jer 29:11). While your journey will look different, and the order in which you tackle life's problems may be different, the end result will be the same: positive, productive, and peaceful relationships with others and a life spent fulfilling God's purpose. I know from personal experience that a life well lived is a life that pleases God. It all starts with belief. Belief that God loves you, has uniquely gifted you, and has a purpose and a plan for you that will impact the people in your life and His Kingdom forever.

three

Being the Woman Leader
Christ Would Pick

*You have been chosen, and you must therefore use
such strength and heart and wits as you have.*
—*J. R. R. Tolkien*

It doesn't happen every week, but I absolutely love it when it does. It brings a smile to my face and a spring to my step. What is it? It is simply when I receive a text from my daughter, who has a break in her college class schedule and a couple of hours to kill.

"Mom, wanna meet me at Chick-fil-A?"

I'll move mountains to say yes as often as I can. Why? Because she picked me! Out of all the people and things (her new husband, shopping, friends, homework), she chose me to "kill" time with!

Getting picked is a wonderful feeling. The intensity of emotion a person can get from being picked is amazing. It is the same intensity level on the negative side when we are not picked. For many of us, the thought of not being chosen or picked for something takes us back to elementary school, when, for whatever sport, two people were designated the captains and began alternately picking people for their teams. It was as if our self-worth was knocked down another notch with each subsequent pick that we weren't chosen. We never wanted to be picked last. To be last meant we were least popular, or worse still, a loser.

Perhaps you're athletic, so being picked for sports wasn't an issue. Perhaps you wanted to be picked to help the teacher in the classroom or some other setting. In retrospect, looking back more objectively, it's likely that it was your gifting or skill level that determined when you were picked and not as much weight put on your popularity as you felt at the time.

As a woman today—whether you're in the home, ministry, or the workplace—when you have a job you need someone to do, you generally pick the person based on one of two criteria: (1) ability and willingness to get the job done or (2) enthusiasm and willingness to learn.

Christ understood those criteria well. He understood that certain qualities are better than others for a specific job. As He picked His inner circle, He had certain character qualities, skills, and talents He was looking for. While it was true for the twelve disciples, I think it was also true for the individuals beyond the twelve who were part of the inner circle who traveled with Him. In Luke 8:1–3, we find that women were part of this inner circle. As we dig into this glimpse of the women Christ picked for His inner circle, we uncover three qualities Christ looked for in women leaders. Some of these qualities you may have, and some you may not. Regardless, your enthusiasm and willingness to learn will determine the trajectory of the future God has for you as a woman leader. Let's take a look at the passage.

> Jesus traveled about from one town and village to another, proclaiming the good news of the Kingdom of God. The Twelve were with him, and also some women who had been cured of evil spirits and diseases: Mary (called Magdalene) from whom seven demons had come out; Joanna the wife of Chuza, the manager of Herod's household; Susanna; and many others. These women were helping to support them out of their own means. (Lk 8:1–3 NIV)

Despite the many leadership lessons throughout the Bible, this excerpt highlights three qualities that were unique for the women in leadership whom Christ allowed access to His inner circle. These three qualities were authenticity, courage, and generosity.

AUTHENTICITY

At this time in history, women were not permitted to be taught by a rabbi. If allowed any education at all, it came directly from a woman's husband. As dictated by tradition, a woman's place was in the home, yet these women were traveling with Jesus, learning from His daily teaching, and living a parallel existence to the famous twelve disciples. The women invited into Christ's inner circle to experience the same teaching as His disciples were authentic. They were real. No masks, no facades. They were willing to be authentic regardless of what people thought. They were more concerned with serving Jesus and receiving all that He had for them than what others might think of their flaws and imperfections. Clearly, Jesus looks for disciples who are authentic. There are several reasons why being authentic is key for the woman leader.

Being Authentic Shows Strength

I started and co-led a group called Becoming a Confident Woman in Leadership. These women and I meet twice a month and learn biblical principles of leadership and fulfilling God's purpose for our lives. While the coleaders and I are regular speakers, the speaking calendar is also filled with women from all walks of life—from moms, to Mary Kay consultants, to managers. On a recent group night, we had a wonderful woman of God whom many in the group knew of and respected. She was seen as a matriarch of the faith, which meant to many people, her life was somehow close to perfect. The topic for the evening was forgiveness and the role it plays on our ability to influence (a.k.a., lead). She came bearing an authentic story of a real-life struggle she was having with her father-in-law, an extremely critical, demanding, and negative man, especially toward her husband, who worked for him.

She shared what life was like for her husband working for his father. We sensed the frustration of her reality when she even cursed, calling her father-in-law an a**. She walked us through her prayers, her methods for continually forgiving him, and how she was putting feet to her faith to show love for a man she really didn't even like. It was a moving message, with which every woman in the room connected. While not everyone had a similar father-in-law, they did have difficulty with forgiveness. Some struggled with a difficulty forgiving others, some with a difficulty forgiving themselves. While they knew she was a woman of faith, her authenticity that came through during that night's message spoke volumes to her strength.

While I'm not encouraging you to pour out your guts about your past hurts, sins, or struggles to every person you meet, being authentic is a powerful testimony to your strength as a woman—a woman leader. Even more important, it's a powerful testimony to the strength of your Savior, Jesus Christ. Authenticity is transparency about those past hurts, struggles, and issues that reveals the internal strength of a woman. People want to follow a leader who is strong. The woman leader reveals that strength through being authentic.

Being Authentic Shows Trust

In general, women have trust issues. Whether it's a result of our being raised by parents who brought disappointment upon disappointment or a more recent betrayal by a spouse or friend, trusting others is challenging to many women. And the more times your confidence has been broken, the more difficult it can be to live authentically. People don't generally follow leaders they don't believe. Yet trust is mutually inclusive—meaning we are open to *trust* others when we feel they are open and trust us. Authenticity is one of the ways we establish confidence with others. Whether we are coming home or heading to Capitol Hill, when we are authentic, we help the people we are leading to be more open and authentic. It eliminates any thoughts of, *She seems to be holding something back. Can I trust her?*

Being Authentic Shows Character

Going back to my friend who spoke of her father-in-law. She could have told any number of stories that she found on the Internet to get her point across about forgiveness.

However, she chose to be authentic (also defined as honest) about a particular circumstance she was dealing with in her own life. Her honesty, particularly in negative circumstances, revealed a great deal about her character.

Pick up any book on leadership and you'll find character to be the number-one quality of a successful leader. When you dig into those character qualities, you find that the leading trait is honesty. By definition, being authentic is being genuine or real (a.k.a., true). While being honest in your relationships, financially, and through other circumstances is important, there is no higher level of authenticity and integrity than being honest with others about yourself.

Being Authentic Honors God

My friend's struggle with her critical father-in-law showed humility, vulnerability, and ultimately, an acknowledgment that she didn't have all the answers. Yet her message pointed us to the One who *does* have the answers, the One who can give us the strength to do difficult things (like forgive) that we don't necessarily want to do. God has carefully knit us together, woven together all the circumstances of our lives, and gifted us with specific gifts and talents—all for His glory. Her authenticity allows us to see a glimpse of God working in her life and using her in a unique way. To try to hide, fit in, or stand out as something we are not is to dishonor His unique design within us. We recognize the beauty of authenticity because it points us to the beauty of our Creator.

COURAGE

The women invited into Christ's inner circle to experience the same teaching as His disciples were courageous. These Luke 8 women were brave because they risked doing what others wouldn't. They were trailblazers willing to risk public ridicule and perhaps even death for attempting to learn from a rabbi—something that was forbidden to those deemed not worthy (women). While Jesus was gracious to and inclusive of these women, it still took a lot of courage to step outside the cultural norm to be and study with Jesus and His disciples. Being courageous is important for women leaders for several reasons.

Being Courageous Shows Belief in Your Calling

I can remember my first experiences with writing. My church was putting together some devotionals to go with a sermon series, and they asked me to write them. Most of my writing had been confined to e-mails, business training, and the like. It had always been about teaching something specific and never really about expressing my own thoughts or ideas on a particular topic. When I was asked, I thought, *Who am I to interpret Scripture? Who am I to bring to life a passage of the Bible?*

I knew God was calling me to write, and I knew I had a knack for writing. My husband and others had nicknamed me "the wordsmith": they could always count on me to express what they wanted to write clearly and succinctly. Yet this new realm of Scripture interpretation made me nervous and apprehensive. I struggled internally, so I'm sure no one knew what I was dealing with, but it took courage for me to step out of my comfort zone and write those devotionals. Did they change anyone's life? I don't know. I never received any comments or letters of life change. Nonetheless, it took a lot of courage to say yes, and one reward was that it put me on the path to God's greater purpose for my life and for His Kingdom.

Another example that comes to mind is the unassuming and modest image of a Scottish woman who took the stage of *Britain's Got Talent* in 2009. Until that day, Susan Boyle had sung only in her church and the local theater of her obscure little village. It was evident in watching the YouTube video of her performance (which received more than ten million views) that no one in the audience that day expected much from her. Yet it was her courage to step out and audition and ultimately sing in front of millions of viewers that launched her onto the path to fulfilling her purpose.

You too were created with talents and abilities. (They may still be diamonds in the rough, but they're there!) Everything has been perfected by God for a purpose—even the silly voices you make when you talk with children! If you believe strongly enough that you were created to speak to audiences, you will be courageous and speak. If you believe you were created to sing, you will be courageous and sing. Whatever you believe about yourself is revealed through your courageous actions.

I could have made a dozen excuses why I couldn't write those devotionals, but it was the courage to follow that faint inkling that God was calling me to write that helped me to tackle the task I really knew so little about at the time. While sometimes the courage is felt more internally than seen externally, it all boils down to your belief in yourself and who God created you to be.

Being Courageous Shows Belief in Others
The truth of this statement is repeated time and time again throughout the Bible and in the life of any modern-day leader. Every hero of Scripture, from Noah, to David, to Esther, to Jesus Himself, stood up with courage against

their adversaries, not just because of the belief in their calling but also because of their belief in others.

Commentary writers mention the ridicule that Noah endured as he labored to build the ark in a time when it had never rained. Yet his faith in God and the belief that he had been called for a purpose to save the lives of his family and the animals were what gave him the courage to persist. David endured exile and many near-death experiences with Saul because he believed in the people of Israel and the vision God had given him on their behalf. Esther risked her life to go before the king without being summoned to save the Jewish people. Jesus left the glorious riches of heaven to live life on earth, enduring all the frailties and pain of existing in a fallen world only to die for us. He did that not for anything He would gain; He already had it all, yet he gave it up so that He could ultimately share His riches and eternal life with us.

Even throughout history, we can look at people who became famous because their belief in others gave them the courage to act: Joan of Arc fought against the English dominion of France for her belief in the people of France and King Charles VII. That deep belief ultimately led her to be burned at the stake in 1431 at the age of nineteen. Rosa Parks endured public ridicule and arrest as she took a stand against segregation because of her deep belief that all races were created equal. Corrie ten Boom endured imprisonment at a concentration camp during World War II for hiding and protecting the Jewish people from death at the hands of the Nazis because she believed every life, regardless of religion or nationality, was a precious gift. These are just a few of a long list of heroes and heroines throughout history who stepped out in courage because of their belief in others.

Regardless of where you are a leader—in your home, your work, or your community—the foundation of your leadership is your belief in others. Whether you believe they deserve a better environment, a better widget, or better drinking water, your courage to step out and take action reveals the value you see in others. Women are called to lead—at home, in their jobs, and yes, even from the pulpit. I have been laughed at and kindly dismissed on more than one occasion for declaring that opinion. Yet it is my strong conviction that women (*you*) and God's ability to use them to do a mighty work in this world have driven me to write this book and to establish the National Association of Christian Women Leaders (you can find out more about NACWL in this book's appendix). What passion are you being courageously called to live out?

Being Courageous Shows Belief in God
Pastor Brady Boyd of New Life Church in Colorado Springs was interviewed by CNN in the aftermath of a shooting that took place at his church in 2007. During that interview he said, "As Christians we were put on this planet to make things right. That there was something each of us was put here to make right." To step out from the crowd—to stand up for something or someone—requires courage. It requires not only that we believe in ourselves and in others, but in the very God who created us. Yes, I believe He equips the called so that we can fulfill our purpose, yet we need Him to help us through every part of the journey. To step courageously into our purpose, we know there will be doors we need opened, people we require the favor of, and financial and other resources that are outside of our control. To move courageously toward that vision shows our

belief in God. It is our belief in His ability, sovereignty, and power to bring that vision to completion.

In 2006 and 2007, God brought our family to its knees. I had felt the call to speak, write, and coach for some time, but frankly, I was comfortable with a great life making great money (I was a financial advisor, and my husband was in the construction business at the time). In a little more than twelve months, we went from flush with cash, full IRAs, no credit card debt, and giving generously to being bankrupt and just trying to hold on to our home.

My husband owned a construction company, and when the real estate bubble burst, the construction business dried up to nothing. Entire communities that were underway sat untouched for years. It was the equivalent of tumbleweeds rolling through the towns of the old west. My husband did any odd jobs and remodels that he could find, but the recession had hit southwest Florida extremely hard. Many construction companies went under, leaving small contractors like my husband holding the bills.

The investment crash came on the heels of the construction crash, which caused my income to plummet. Southwest Florida is primarily a senior retiree market, so my clients wanted to cash in whatever was left of their investments for fear they wouldn't outlive their retirement money. As an advisor I didn't make an income for holding cash; my income came from investing their money, which they were unwilling to do. I couldn't blame them—I wasn't comfortable investing it myself.

Financial struggles are scary. And often my family and I wondered what God was doing in our lives. Yet deep down, I knew. God was doing for me what I couldn't do for myself:

thrusting me out of my comfortable, well-paying career to pursue His purpose for my life. When I had not been able to say no to the comfort and money my career provided and say yes to God and His plan, God painfully removed that obstacle.

Yet I still had a choice. I could have scrambled to get more clients in a volatile financial environment. I could have looked to switch careers and find a salaried profession that would get our family through. Or I could trust God and start the journey to discover the purpose my writing, speaking, and coaching were meant to fulfill. I can tell you I would never have chosen that path had it not been for my strong belief in God and the greater purpose I knew He had for me—even though at the time it wasn't clear what that purpose was.

God has been faithful to provide in every way. We never missed a meal. Though late at times, we never missed paying the mortgage, electric bill, or other necessity. He kept our cars running and our bodies healthy. While there is still much uncertainty about my future path as a writer and founder of the National Association of Christian Women Leaders, I awake each day and courageously take the next step God gives me to help women fulfill their calling and reach their highest potential as a leader.

GENEROSITY

I recently attended a Chick-fil-A Leadercast. It's an annual event in which Chick-fil-A organizers bring in key leaders to talk about leadership. Throughout the day, almost without exception, the speakers talked about adding value as a leader. The bottom line was that you can't be a successful leader if you're not adding value to others—in other words, giving them something they don't already have. Yet as the day drew to a close, I thought I would take the opportunity to ask a few people, "What is it that you have received when you walk away from time with a leader that makes you think, *Wow, they really added value to my life today!*" Surprisingly, most didn't have an answer. While every speaker told of how important it was to add value as a leader, not a single leader I talked to understood what that meant.

I have thought a lot about that question since asking it that day. And I connected it with this question: What does all this have to do with Jesus picking these women leaders? Jesus didn't pick these women just because they were giving to his ministry. No, He could see their hearts. These women were leaders Christ picked because He understood the real meaning of being a leader who adds value. Truth is, as a leader you can't add value to someone unless you *give* him or her something he or she does not already have. Being generous is the key ingredient to adding value.

Being Generous Adds Value through Giving Knowledge

I recently read an article on the social media phenomenon Pinterest ("Why Is Pinterest a $2.5 Billion Company?," *Forbes*). As it turns out, this four-year-old start-up has *not* generated an ounce of revenue to date, yet it is currently valued at $2.5 billion. Yes, that's billion with a *B*! Why, you ask? Basically, it boils down to knowledge.

In a unique and fascinating way, by capturing your attention with images, Pinterest delivers knowledge. While you may think it's only a place where you can waste hours getting fit without breaking a sweat or cook delicious meals without setting foot in the kitchen, the truth is, Pinterest is currently the number-one destination for knowledge seekers. And the knowledge comes in more than thirty distinct categories, from architecture to women's fashion. You can learn anything from gardening techniques or how to avoid bears while camping to how to use proper lighting or turn the pictures on your phone into professional-looking images. It is because Pinterest adds so much value that it is currently pulling away from the pack as the leader in social media.

There is a knowledge that you bring to the world. Although it may not necessarily be what you believe is a unique knowledge, the delivery of it *is* unique to you and you alone. And it's a knowledge that individuals in your circle of influence are seeking. When you become generous in sharing the knowledge you have with others, you become a leader.

Being Generous Adds Value through Giving Resources
Time, material goods, and money are all resources we can be generous with. I believe it is this combination and this ability to add value that Christ sees so readily in women that targets them for leadership in His Kingdom. How many times have you heard a stay-at-home mom heading back into the workforce say, "Why would an employer hire me? I don't have any work experience." Yet this same stay-at-home mom will see a friend who checks out of the hospital and in a split second whip up a meal to deliver to her and help her with things while she visits. It is this fast decision-making ability that determines using time, physical, and financial resources to meet the needs of others that raises this mom to leadership status. In this seemingly automatic decision, this

woman has become a leader who adds value through the giving of her resources.

Being Generous Adds Value through Giving Encouragement

I've coached women from all over the country, and regardless of the stress, struggle, or challenge they face, I always find them to be encouraging. Perhaps it stems from the paradigm that we give that which we need the most. Regardless, many women are natural encouragers—which I believe further equips them to be natural leaders as well. Sure, you can gather a team, a tribe, or an army and pump them up with a grand vision or goal, but it takes encouragement to keep them going when the road gets tough. And regardless of who you're leading, rough times always come. The teams that stay the course despite opposition or oppression are those that get regular doses of encouragement.

My suspicion is that because you've picked up this book and have read this far, you are eager and willing to fulfill God's purpose for your life. In the next chapters, we will unpack the three areas in the new Personal Growth Map that help develop women leaders; why they work in developing you as the authentic, courageous, and generous leader God picks; and why the time is now to step into your calling of leadership.

four

Becoming a Confident Woman
in Leadership

Without continual growth and progress, such words as
improvement, achievement, and success have no meaning.
—*Benjamin Franklin*

Apple updates its iOS (its mobile operating system) at least once a year. Regardless of where you fall in the smartphone war—Android or iPhone—you certainly can't argue that the research and development (R&D) at these companies is unbelievable. Many consumers have barely scratched the surface of what their smartphones can accomplish before the next version hits the market.

Apple spends millions of dollars and hours making sure that the product it delivers meets the needs of its customers. Apple also works to exceed its own expectations and even what it understands the customers' needs to be! As a result, according to *Engadget* (an online technology publication), Apple reported $36 billion in revenue and $8.2 billion in net profit in 2012.

Now take that same R&D mentality and apply it to your church's women's ministry. When was the last time your women's ministry was updated to more fully develop women to their highest potential (leadership)?

While women's ministry may not be a financial profit-making endeavor, its lack of profit focus is the very reason this area (product line, if you will) in most churches is going out of business. Google "women's ministry," and you will find hundreds of articles about all the things that are wrong with it, why churches aren't even bothering to start them, and any other number of negative-slanted issues. Yet check out Amazon and you won't find one book offering help for creating an effective women's ministry. You may find fifty options that come up when you put "women's ministry" in the search engine of your favorite bookseller. Scan the results, however, and you'll discover there really isn't anything about the organization itself or its effective function. Merely fifty book options that you might want to consider incorporating into your women's ministry. Likely good options, but random at best when it comes to meeting the needs of a woman. And I can guarantee that if you asked Apple, LG, or any other major business how "random" affects their profits, you'll find it doesn't work at all. In fact, it's unlikely any aspect of their products is random.

So if Apple and other great companies can profit from being intentional in their product offering, can the church? Specifically, can the church be intentional as it relates to women's ministry and developing women into strong leaders? Of course it can! The question is not "Can the church profit?" but "*What* does it profit?" The answer—*a lot.*

It's easy for companies like Apple to be intentional because it knows its purpose (to be the leader in technology innovation) and the purpose of its individual products. Churches, on the other hand, don't have a unified purpose for their women (beyond salvation, generally speaking). So they are left to shoot in the dark about what women need. They can target the suffering pieces of women's lives but tend to lose sight beyond that. As women, we feel there has to be something more to this Christian life than "just" salvation. We wonder, *What about me? What's my purpose? Is serving on Sunday morning really all there is? I feel like I was made for something greater, yet I don't know where to start to find it.* Sadly, with women's ministries on the decline, and with many of the existing ministries failing to adequately address those wonderings, many women realize—as I did—that the answer may not be found inside the walls of the church.

As we outlined in the previous chapters, every Christian (women included) is called to fulfill God's highest potential for his or her life: leadership. Yet as women, we know that looks different for each of us. Some are moms, some work in ministry, and some work in the secular workplace. Although we are each different, the question is the same: How do I discover my purpose and fulfill my highest calling to leadership? That's where the Personal Growth Map comes in, and that's where we turn our attention in this chapter.

Discovering a Woman's Needs

In the first chapter, I mentioned how God provided the details of the map, and a solid group of women leaders fleshed out the resources for each category. As we began to work on the map—which, in summary, covered three categories (Moving On, Moving Up, and Moving Out)—we discovered it encompassed more than thirty topics and hundreds of resources. It seemed overwhelming to implement.

So when you can't do it all, you start small. Which is just what we did.

We decided to launch Becoming a Confident Woman in Leadership, a group that helps women embrace their call to leadership and understand the importance of their ability to influence (lead) those in their circles. (Read the appendix for more details.) Within a year of establishing and promoting the group, I received confirmation of the map and clarity regarding its implementation.

Aware of my passion for women in leadership, my experience in coaching women, and my knack for analyzing information to get to the heart of the matter, a member of the lead team for an association of churches asked me to review a collection of information they had gathered from the women serving in ministry within their association. The information included results of several surveys they had conducted with these women as well as a long list of questions that the women had presented to the leaders at a recent conference. The goal of the organization was to help discover what these women needed so that they could actively support them as they ministered to others in their churches.

When I looked over the data and finished my analysis, I sat in awe at seeing God's hand at work. I had picked apart the data and categorized the findings to learn, with just a few exceptions, that the needs of the women of this organization were the exact same needs of women as a whole—something God had revealed to me a year earlier with the Personal Growth Map for women. It made perfect sense: while our outer circumstances might be different, our inner needs are still the same. You may have a group of pastors' wives, a group of entrepreneurs, and a group of housewives, yet at the core, they are all women. The outer influences (stresses, hurts, challenges) may be different, but the tools they need to survive, thrive, and serve their purpose for God are the same.

While at that time I didn't know what God intended me to do with this knowledge, I was certain of one thing: God had provided the map of personal growth for what women need to reach their highest potential. He had provided it, and less than a year later, He confirmed it. As a writer and speaker, I knew the first step was to get the concepts in print for others to read and understand. It wasn't until several months later, when I was asked to speak to a local Mothers of Preschoolers (MOPS) chapter, that I felt in my spirit that this needed to be an organization to help women follow the map to their highest potential, as well as to partner with churches to provide the resources they needed to help their women fulfill their purpose. It was too large for one church to implement effectively, but bringing women together across the country and even in communities could make it possible. And after much prayer, research, and encouragement from the original team, I decided to establish the National Association of Christian Women Leaders (more on this in the appendix).

It seemed that everything God had given me started and ended with the Personal Growth Map. It was how I went from surviving to thriving. Through it I had discovered my greater purpose, and it was this greater joy that I want to share with you and the women you influence. It's a map for how each of us can—despite our pasts, our hurts, and our struggles—discover who God created us to be and walk in the fullness of our gifting. We are not just to be women who admire the Beth Moores and Joyce Meyers of the world; we are meant to discover *for ourselves* the fulfillment of the one thing we long for: our God-given purpose in life.

You Are a Woman Empowered by God

As I walk you through the Personal Growth Map, you'll notice that it is laid out in a somewhat linear fashion. That is primarily for ease of reading and understanding. However, please note that our progression through it will likely weave back and forth, much like God weaves the tapestry of our lives. While there are reasons for progressing step-by-step (which I will address), you'll find that as God brings your purpose (the Moving Out section below) to new levels, you will likely revisit parts of the Moving On and Moving Up categories. Each time God will take you to new areas of growth, greater freedom, and a deeper peace and trust in Him.

So without further ado, I present the Personal Growth Map. The map is designed to help guide you through the areas that are holding you back from reaching your highest potential, to help you move on from past struggles, to move up by equipping you in areas needed, and to move out into the purpose and plan God has for your life. I labeled the map We[G] for Women Empowered by God. While each of our individual journeys through the map is unique, it is the unity of all of us serving God's greater purpose that brings us together. As you walk through each of the map's three categories, you'll see how the historical division among women based on what you do (mom, career woman, ministry leader) begins to fade from focus, and your attention is drawn to who you are becoming as a woman of God—the beautiful and strong woman leader He has called you to be.

Plagued

It's easiest to see on reality TV these days, but if you look around for it, you'll notice it in the lives of other women and even yourself at some point (perhaps even now). It's that feeling that your life is plagued. Plagued with problems, drama, insecurities, and chaos. Problems at work, at home, everywhere you turn, it seems. Conflict is a normal occurrence in relationships, so when you are often offended, you may regularly think, *If they would...do this...not do that...then...*

The woman who feels continually plagued by life's problems is best suited for the Moving On category. If I were to sum up all the attributes of this phase in one word, it would be *unhealthy*. In other words, physically, emotionally, mentally, and/or spiritually (sometimes it's one area, but oftentimes all the areas are interwoven and connected), a person is unhealthy. The Moving On category is about seeking healing, health, and wholeness for women who need to overcome pains and struggles. The Moving On category helps women begin to walk confidently in who they are and experience the freedom in life Christ provides. Areas for growth include the following.

Moving On

1. Loss (death, divorce, and abandonment)
2. Abuse (of all kinds)
3. Health/Diet
4. Addictions and Disorders
5. Establishing Healthy Boundaries
6. Self-esteem (identity in Christ)
7. Basics of Christian Faith/Spiritual Disciplines
8. Spiritual Roadblocks (removing unforgiveness, worry, doubt, bitterness, etc.)

Not Plagued but Perplexed

As we begin to heal and escape from those things that have held us back and kept us hostage (Moving On), we are able to see potential and a brighter future filled with the opportunities God has placed before us. While chaos can still be present when we enter this next stage, Moving Up, it generally stems not from unhealthy relationships but from poor habits or lack of discipline.

Symptoms in this category include feeling overwhelmed, stressed, and perhaps even burned out. These symptoms aren't a result of any particular relationship but a result of the sheer volume of what we are trying to accomplish on any given day. The Moving Up category helps us get it together so that we can focus on maintaining balance, discover our purpose, and strengthen mind, body, and spirit. Growth in these areas allows us to walk courageously and unencumbered into the call of leadership God has for us. These growth areas include the following.

Moving Up
1. Self-care, Time Management and Organization Skills
2. Financial Management
3. Personality, Strengths and Purpose Discovery
4. Thought Management
5. Effective Self-leadership
6. Effective Communication Skills (including handling conflict and boundaries)

Free to Lead

Once we grasp our goals and purpose, we can begin to live those out and minister to others who need encouragement, challenge, and help finding their own purpose. The

Moving Out section provides encouragement and support for women who are moving out into the areas where God has called and equipped them to lead. Mainly, these areas of leadership are as follows.

Moving Out

1. Business
2. Local Church
3. Local Community or Neighborhood
4. International Missions
5. Home

While the above are in no particular order—and depending on your phase of life, you could fall in multiple or different areas—the point of the Moving Out category is that you are serving where God has called you. While you may or may not feel that where you are is your life's purpose, it *is* your purpose during this season. And regardless of what area you serve, you need support, encouragement, and inspiration to continue serving at full capacity.

The Importance of Moving On

Twice in the New Testament (Mark 5 and Luke 8), the person Christ heals asks if he can join Him in ministry. In both instances, Christ directs the person to go home. It is understandable why someone healed of demons or a serious illness as these two passages record would jump for joy and desire to join in the ministry of the man who delivered such a miracle. Yet in His wisdom, Christ asks that they go home. While He doesn't give a lengthy explanation of His command, as we ponder the life of a sick person, it becomes clear. Even with complete and perfect healing, the ravages of a life of illness take their toll. The mind, body, and spirit are weak. The now whole and healthy person will need to establish healthy routines to gain strength and stamina.

It is likely, if you have suffered with any kind of lengthy illness, that your finances, your home life, your relationships, and even your occupation have been damaged by that illness. It's likely the life you lived as a sick person is not the same life you will live as a healthy person. Discovering who you truly are and what your God-given potential is as a new and whole woman in Christ is a crucial part of the Moving On phase of your journey. Regardless of whether your encounter with Christ is one of physical healing, mental healing, spiritual healing, or something else, there are likely to be many hurts and pains from the past that you must first move on from.

The cliché "hurting people hurt people" is so true. Christ did not send healed people straight into ministry because He knew that they needed strengthening and self-discovery in terms of their pains and hurts before they could effectively minister to others. While individuals can effectively serve in task-oriented ministry, such as greeting, administrative functions, etc., the deeper work of ministry through relationships will be much more productive for the Kingdom when we take the time to understand our past, establish a healthy present, and set about the task of discovering our purpose.

We all have something in our past that we need to face and find healing from. Some issues are bigger or more serious than others. Some require intense healing and forgiveness. But for us to become everything God desires, we must face the past, acknowledge it, and determine to overcome it. Left unresolved, the areas targeted in the Moving On category will stand as an invisible barrier between you and the purpose and plans God has for you. This invisible barrier consists of fears, doubts, negative self-talk, and coping habits so ingrained you consider them a normal part of life. Though you can't see or touch them, they are there, and without effectively moving on from them, you are unable to fulfill your highest potential and God's purpose for your life.

The Power of Moving Up

Once we have gathered our strength, thrown off the burdensome thoughts, habits, and relationships of the past, it's time to get it together. Time to get our house in order, as the Scripture often puts it. Through the Moving On phase, we have discovered who we are *not* based on our past mistakes or circumstances but based on who we *are* in Christ. Now we focus on getting organized so that we can spend time discovering why God has put us on this planet. We discover our personality, our strengths, our passions, and our purpose, and we begin to walk into the ministry path God has for us.

Can we skip this step and do ministry? Absolutely—many do. Yet if we haven't gotten it together, established balance and an adequate margin in key areas, and discovered our true purpose, then our ministry work will likely leave us feeling overwhelmed, frustrated, inadequate, and ineffective. It's the reason we see people who start in a particular ministry quickly burn out and often stop altogether. Adding more to a life that is already full and lacking margin and organization are great ways for the enemy to discourage and disrupt any attempts we make at serving. In addition, if we have not discovered our purpose, it is likely that our first choice of ministry will not suit our personality and gifting for the long haul. Thus, when the excitement wanes, we find ourselves on the sidelines—ineffective, angry, tired, hurt, and disillusioned. Exactly where the enemy would like God's people.

What about where you are serving right now? Overall, are you feeling fulfilled or frustrated? A nagging ongoing sense of frustration is a key sign that you might be serving but not necessarily within God's purpose for you. Are you overwhelmed or approaching burnout? What might be out of balance such that you need to pause for a time so that you can get it together and serve with greater fervor and effectiveness?

The Reward of Moving Out

The ministry we find ourselves in can change. There are times where we may begin our journey ministering in our home and end it ministering in a home on some faraway continent. Yet regardless of our phase of life, we will see the common thread of who we are and God's purpose for us running through every area of ministry in which we serve.

I have an exercise that I take my coaching clients through that helps them discover their life's mission statement. The neat thing about this exercise is that it really gets to core values and people's passions, which means that they have more clarity when they make decisions about ministries and opportunities in which to lead. Just to give you an example, my mission statement is "to discover, create, and inspire freedom for women and their families." Though I did not realize it at the time, during my career in the financial industry, I was fulfilling this vision. I was helping individuals (not just women) create financial freedom. As I moved into life coaching, the freedom that I desired to help women create became more expansive than just finances. I wanted to give them freedom of time and freedom of peace (which I wrote about in my first book, *Freedom from Worry: Prayer of Peace for an Anxious Mind*), and even as I write this book, that mission is expanding further. I want to inspire women and provide them with the tools to discover and create a life of freedom.

United as Women

The beauty of these three categories is that through pursuing them, every woman can grow and live a fulfilled life. They do not segregate us by age, occupation, marital status, or parental status. No longer will we label women: she's a career woman, she's just a stay-at-home mom, she's old, she's young, she's single, she's married. Instead we will look at each other just as God looks at us—as women. Crafted with unique gifts, a unique story that includes pains, trials, and struggles, but all purposed for God's unique plan.

In the Moving On category, you might find a college student, a single mom of two kids, a married woman with no kids, and a grandmother all seeking to regain health after difficult pasts. No longer are they segregated by demographic categories; they are now united by their humanness. The diversity of the group adds richness and the beauty of the experience of women of all ages and walks of life experiencing God's healing and wholeness. Even while focusing on the same area, women of different ages can learn from one another's experiences. Instead of trying to force Titus 2:4 mentoring relationships (the older women must train the younger women), they begin to flow more naturally as we bring women together around their interest in similar areas of personal growth.

The same is true for Moving Up and Moving Out. It's no longer about what we do, but who we are: women leaders becoming authentic, courageous, and generous and living out the purpose and plan God has for them. Stay-at-home moms, single women, and working women brought together to grow in areas that affect every woman—things like conflict management, thought-life management, and effective leadership. These areas aren't bound by age or demographics. All women together can work on the areas that fall in these categories.

As you ponder the concepts of this chapter, you will likely sense in your spirit where the work needs to begin. Do you feel as though you keep running into an invisible wall? Begin praying about what God would have you do in the Moving On category. Are you serving, but like the plate spinner at the circus, you are expecting a plate to come crashing down any minute? Where in the Moving Up category could you make strides to become more effective? In coaching I find that most women often know exactly what it is they need to be doing; it's not lack of knowledge but more lack of urgency. In the next chapter, I want to talk about that and why the time to get moving is *now*.

I encourage you to pray over the Personal Growth Map. Where is the Holy Spirit prompting you to start? Once you have your mind set on your starting point (dealing with loss, getting more organized, discovering your personality, etc.), then begin asking the Holy Spirit to guide you to the resources He has for you. It may be a small group at your church, a workshop being offered in your community, or an online resource at National Association of Christian Women Leaders, Inc. However the Spirit prompts, get busy! There is a lot at stake! In the final chapter, we will unpack why the time to start is now.

five

Why Now Is the Time

*We are [God's] workmanship, created in Christ
Jesus for good works, which God prepared before-
hand so that we would walk in them.*
—*Ephesians 2:10 NASB*

I remember the first time God brought the growing influence of women to my attention. It's crazy to think that it
was more than a decade ago. I lived in southwest Florida
and was working at a leading bank. I received notice from
my manager that I would be attending a new sales training
launch regarding women and investing. *What?* I thought,
surprised. *Really?* That seemed like an odd topic for sales
training.

At that time southwest Florida was home of the newly
wed and the nearly dead (a.k.a., retirees). And since the
young marrieds (myself included) had more debt than
money, my focus for selling the bank's investment products
was on the nearly dead category. My daily goal was to get
in front of these elderly couples and convince them that
doing business with the nation's largest bank was in their

best interest. These sweet couples had been married more than forty years and were from an era that taught that the man took care of the wife, which included all their financial decisions.

Though the wives were in those meetings, they were silent partners. They didn't make any decisions, and most didn't even understand what was happening with their money! They were there to establish a relationship with the banker so that when the husband passed away, they would know whom to turn to for help.

So with that background, I was perplexed as to why I needed training on women and investing. Fortunately, the training was fascinating. The leaders filled each session with statistics on how influential women are in making household decisions, how they manage their money, and what we needed to understand about the coming wealth transfer that would make women the expected recipients of trillions of dollars because of the death of their parents and/or their spouses in the next few decades.

As I listened and took copious amounts of notes, I realized all this change appeared as if God was taking much of what had been earned by men and handing it to women.

What are you up to, God? I wondered. *Why are you doing this?*

After that two-day training session, I returned to my job, enthusiastic about all I had learned but unable to implement most of it because the demographics of my clientele hadn't changed. But I couldn't shake that feeling that God was doing something in the midst of all this wealth. And that feeling hasn't changed.

For more than a decade, I've continued to watch the rising role of women's influence in the world, and I've regularly questioned God about it. *Is this part of a larger movement? What's the big picture?* Each time I keep coming back to the idea that God has started a movement, and we are on the verge of something great.

What Is a Movement?

Movements are tricky to identify until after they've passed and become a part of the history books. Movements generally begin small and gain momentum quickly. Some movements leave our world better off—such as the industrial movement, which brought power-driven machinery like the automobile—and some leave our world in worse shape—think about the Nazis. Regardless of the results, we can trust that our God is using *everything* that happens in this world to bring to fulfillment His greater plan—even when the results of a movement seem to contradict His ultimate plan for eternity in heaven. Whether or not we actually participate in a particular movement, our lives are ultimately changed. For instance, the culture in which we live has been changed by the abolition of slavery, the civil rights movement, and the women's rights movement. Each started with a small number of individuals yet has grown to become a part of the very fabric of our lives.

As I have researched how movements have developed throughout history, I have found that each one follows a pattern in which at least three things take place: (1) human and material resources are united and mobilized; (2) the united individuals exert influence against a specific wrong in the world (e.g., the Civil War ending slavery, the Civil Rights Movement of the 1960s ending segregation based on race, and the Women's Suffrage Movement of the 1920s giving women the right to vote); and (3) those exercising their influence increase their pressure through relentless campaigning and the growth of their size until those resisting succumb to the change.

Are We at the Eve of Another Movement?

I believe that since that training session more than a decade ago, God has definitely been up to something—and that "something" continues to intensify. While I am not certain *what* the movement is, I *am* certain it is taking place. I am also certain that God is calling Christian women to play a great role in it, and that whatever the outcome is, God will ultimately fulfill His plan to redeem the world.

Why do I believe this? Because I see those three "prerequisites" I listed above aligning in our world today. Just take a look at some of these statistics.

1. *Mobilizing human and material resources.* God has begun a shift of financial resources (see statistics below) into the hands of women, along with giving them—almost solely—the ability to decide how they are spent. Imagine the change women could make in the world for God's Kingdom if we were united and mobilized together to fight the injustices that He has placed us here to fight.

- Women age fifty and older control a net worth of $19 trillion and own more than three-fourths of America's financial wealth (*Marketing to Women Quick Facts*, She-conomy.com).

- Over the next decade, women will control two-thirds of consumer wealth in the United States and be the beneficiaries of the largest transference of wealth in our country's history. Estimates range from $12 to $40 trillion. Many boomer women will experience a double inheritance windfall—gaining a financial foothold from both their parents and their husbands ("Marketers Should Not Ignore the She-conomy," EMSI Inc.).

- The number of wealthy women investors in the United States is growing at a faster rate than that of men. In a two-year period, the number of wealthy women in the United States grew by 68 percent while the number of men grew only 36 percent ("Women, Wealth and Power: The Emerging Paradigm," *Forbes*).

2. *Exerting external influence* (market, sway opinion, influence). The influence of women is growing. Yet are we as Christian women uniting and using our influence in ways that advance God's work? Just look at these statistics.

- Women were 53 percent of the electoral vote in the 2012 presidential election ("Election Results," CNN.com).

- Women account for more than 85 percent of all consumer spending decisions ("Top 30 Stats You Need to Know When Marketing to Women," TheNextWeb.com).

- According to the Women Give 2012 Report from the Center of Philanthropy at Indiana University, women give to charity 89 percent more than their male counterparts.

3. *Mounting resistance to counterpressures* (beat the opposition or the competition). While it is less clear what this would be, I find it interesting that as I write this chapter, the United States is fighting ISIS, a radical Muslim group that has quickly begun to dominate the Middle East. ISIS (or ISIL) and the region of the world from which they originate treat women barbarically: forcing women to

cover themselves from head to toe, with a mesh covering even their eyes; forbidding women from going outside of their homes without a male escort; and raping them and performing brutal genital mutilation. While resisting or beating the opposition of such an evil group may seem a bigger, more dangerous job than perhaps you and I are called to, resisting evil and fighting the injustices in our own neighborhoods is definitely something we are called to. After all, the Old Testament prophet Micah summed it up well when he stated, "What does the LORD require of you but to do justice…" (Mi 6:8 NASB).

A few other statistics I find interesting, which also indicate to me that there is a greater movement of God going on:

- The US Bureau of the Census (www.census.gov) reports that women currently outnumber men by six million.
- On any given Sunday, thirteen million more adult women than men attend America's churches ("Quick Facts," ChurchforMen.com).
- Midweek church activities often draw 70 to 80 percent female participants ("Quick Facts," ChurchforMen.com).

While these statistics are empowering for women, they also point out an important truth: with power comes great responsibility. We can remain isolated in our own little world, and we can likely make a small dent. We can take the money God has blessed us with and keep it tucked away for our own use. But that isn't what God is calling us to do. Think about what we could accomplish if we came together as women of faith, joining God's movement to impact the injustices of the world and bring glory to His Kingdom. Part of being a great leader and influencer is knowing how best to unite with others and how best to use the funds and other resources God has put in our hands.

A Successful Movement Requires Being Willing to Lead

As I look at the many areas of responsibility for women to dive into, I find that most women aren't "diving." Women leaders are either too hard, trying to copy some of their male counterparts, or they are too soft, not knowing how to lead authentically from a position of confidence in who they are or the goals they wish to achieve. Add to that a growing leadership crisis in the country. In a *Forbes* article, Mike Myatt wrote, "We don't have enough leaders nor do we have a sufficient training strategy to develop leaders" ("A Crisis of Leadership: What's Next?"). And a look across the leadership spectrum makes it obvious that our world could use godly leaders—and in particular, godly *women* leaders! Yet we can have all the money in the world, and we still won't lead people to Christ if we first aren't leading.

Historically women have been on the sidelines, either by choosing to sit quietly in their comfort zones or by engaging only to be dismissed by men based on the culture of the day. Regardless of how we have found ourselves out of play, it has left men shouldered with the heavy leadership load. While in some arenas a woman's leadership call may look different from a man's, the principles are the same. It's not until we move on and move up that we can move out by combining leadership principles with our purpose to fulfill the greater work that God has planned for each of us.

Throughout the pages of this book, we've discovered that God's call for women leaders is clear; thus, we need to focus on what's missing. How do we lead confidently without being too hard or too soft?

A Successful Movement Requires Using Your Influence

Your influence is not a skill you must acquire. You already have it! Women have long been known for their influence. It started with Eve in the Garden of Eden. How easily she influenced Adam to eat the forbidden fruit. Unfortunately, that influence led to her losing her home in the garden. Throughout the pages of Scripture, we see over and over women using their influence—both for good and for bad! Long before leadership was a hot topic, these women were leading. Some used their negative influences: Eve, Herodias (who had John the Baptist's head cut off), and Jezebel (a wicked queen over Israel). Others used their influence for good: Esther (who saved her entire race), Hannah (who dedicated her son Samuel to the Lord), and Ruth (a foreigner who loved her mother-in-law, Naomi, and worked hard to feed her, landing Ruth in the genealogy of Jesus).

We know that these biblical women weren't "special." They remind each of us that we too have influence and are called to use it. Our choice is whether we'll use our influence as women leaders for the positive or negative? And it's not just about our influence individually. Imagine our influence if we were united! Our society has done a wonderful job separating and isolating women, putting us neatly in our own self-described boxes. There's the stay-at-home-mom box, the career-woman box, the Baptist box, the Catholic box, the single box, the married box. And each box contains a woman who is stressed and fighting the battles of her own little boxes instead of fighting the greater evils on earth in order to build God's Kingdom. What roles of influence do you currently have? How are you being intentional with that influence to impact the world? Are you joining other women to influence?

A Successful Movement Requires Fighting Opposition

Although opposition can mean many things in the realm of business and government—competition, for instance—opposition has a clear meaning for Christians. It is about fighting evil in all its forms—from the "big evils," such as hunger, poverty, or sex trafficking, to the more insidious ones, such as pride, deceit, or hatred.

As God began to open my eyes toward the many ways we are called to fight opposition, He provided me with two solid examples of ways we can become involved.

The first came when I met a precious eightysomething woman of God who had been serving the Lord around the world for several decades with her ministry, WOW International. As we talked, she told me a story about Nigerian widows. In some remote places in Nigeria, women are blamed when their husbands die. Not only are they blamed for the death, but they are also punished severely. Their heads are shaved (a symbol of shame), all their possessions are confiscated by male in-laws, they are forced to drink the water that the dead corpses were bathed in, and then they are kicked out of their homes, left to fend for themselves on the streets.

I cannot imagine being a grieving widow and having to endure such added torture. I couldn't get the story out of my mind. It infuriated me that women would be treated this way for no reason. This practice is an evil cultural mindset that no one has stood in opposition to prevent. It is likely no one has stood against it because the punishment for such opposition would be even more degrading, if not deadly. Yet I knew it would be difficult to stand up for these sisters around the world when we often don't stand up for our mistreated sisters on our own soil. It's easy to turn a blind eye to what goes on across the world when we turn a blind eye to what happens on our own streets.

The second story came a couple of months later and made national news. On May 15, 2014, a twenty-seven-year-old, pregnant Sudanese woman, Meriam Yahya Ibrahim, was sentenced to one hundred lashes for adultery (even though she was legally married to a Christian man) and then to death by hanging for the crime of apostasy. She could be "forgiven" if she renounced her Christian faith. Ibrahim, a physician who graduated from the University of Khartoum Medical School, refused.

Since she was almost nine months pregnant when she was arrested, the courts were "lenient" and ruled to allow her to live long enough to give birth and wean her child. Fortunately, the public outrage that resulted from the media attention this story received ensured her release. Yet how many such cases have happened in the past that no one has risen up against?

For more than a week, I pondered and prayed about these women and other women around the world who were suffering similar tragedies. And what kept surprising me was that with each thought and prayer, God seemed to connect those situations with His call to raise up Christian women leaders. But I wasn't sure how.

As I continued to pray, God began to fill my mind with a phrase: *a rising tide.* Though I wasn't sure what that phrase meant, I was sure I had heard the expression before. Sure enough, with a quick Google search, I discovered how I'd heard it.

In 1963, President John F. Kennedy gave a speech that promoted the idea that improvements in the general economy would benefit all participants in that economy. And he said, "A rising tide lifts all boats."

That's when the connection became clear. I believe God was teaching me that by raising up women leaders—building their dignity, their self-respect, and their confidence—I would also help to raise up the dignity and the respect for *all* women around the world. In a sense, it's contagious.

We were created to abolish these injustices and save the world through Christ. All the pieces of the movement are here: women with a deep desire to discover their greater purpose and to embrace all that God has created them to be. Women who have the financial resources, the ability to influence, and who understand the opposition to be defeated. The only thing missing is the training and the troop motivation—which is the purpose of this book. To give you to a fuller understanding of the beautiful woman God has created you to be. To help you comprehend the role your past hurts and struggles play in strengthening you. To bring together women, just like you, to support one another in this journey and not to tear one another down. To provide you with a road map for moving on from your past and with tools for getting your life together so that you can grasp and move up and out to fully embrace God's call on your life.

Now What?

A few years ago, as I began to more intentionally seek my purpose in this movement, I found myself no longer asking God, "What are You doing? Why are You doing it?" Instead, my questions evolved: "What do You want *me* to do? What is my role in Your greater plans?"

As I listened for His response, I began to feel a deep passion for helping women, as I've mentioned above. I knew that was God's answer for me. So I have pursued uniting women for the cause of Christ, helping them grow into their calling, and supporting them as they change the world for God's Kingdom. Part of that pursuit has included writing this book. Another part is launching the National Association of Christian Women Leaders (see the appendix for additional details on what it is and how you can get involved or get more resources for your own pursuits).

Since I've discovered and begun to passionately and purposefully pursue God's calling on my life, I've experienced more joy and peace than I ever could have imagined. I'm so glad I said yes to breaking away from the low expectations of our society and growing my influence to become the best leader I can be.

Now what about you? Do you sense God moving? Are you asking God, "What are You doing? Why are You doing this, God?" Or have you moved, as I did, to the next question: "What's my place in this movement?" I believe (from personal experience) that you'll find great fulfillment and purpose when you stop asking God what He's doing and start asking Him what He wants *you* to do and where He wants you to lead. Whether it's leading from your home by influencing your children to grow up to love and follow Jesus or leading in the workplace or a ministry, leadership is the calling.

Are you willing to pursue that calling and grow personally and as a leader? Are you willing to take on this great adventure to experience a journey beyond your wildest imaginings?

You have been called to lead. You. Really.

So don't put it off another day. People in your home, on your street, in your city, and around the world are counting on *you* to help raise the tide.

Appendix

Next Steps: National Association of Christian Women Leaders, Inc.

Throughout this book, we've looked at our calling and our leadership potential. Now it's time to consider some possible next steps. As I wrote, I felt God calling me to found an organization that would bring women from all walks of life together, grow them as leaders, and offer them the opportunity to unify as we work together to build God's Kingdom. That organization has become the National Association of Christian Women Leaders (NACWL).

As you pray about your possible next steps, I hope you'll consider getting involved in this exciting new organization that's dedicated to *you* and your leadership needs.

The National Association of Christian Women Leaders exists to:

Unite Women—Grow Leaders—Fight Injustice

Uniting women. NACWL believes in uniting women of faith. We believe that as women, we are stronger together than divided. We believe that individually, we may be mother, entrepreneur, career woman, community volunteer, international missionary, or minister in the local church, but together we are a mighty throng ("The Lord announces the word, and the women who proclaim it are a mighty throng," Ps 68:11). We believe we do not serve ourselves, others, or God when we separate ourselves by age, income, education, race, religious denomination, or marital status. But we do when we unite ourselves as women of the Most High God, fashioned for His purpose for such a time as this.

Growing leaders. We believe that as women, when we are authentic and come together to focus on God and the areas of needed growth to fulfill His highest call of leadership (a.k.a., influence), then all comparisons, jealousy, and envy fade away. Whether our influence is in a room of sticky little faces or in the boardroom, our call to influence the world for Christ is the same. We believe in inspiring, encouraging, and facilitating personal growth in women.

Fighting injustice. We believe, as President John F. Kennedy stated, "A rising tide lifts all boats." And when we as women of faith rise up as leaders, the injustices against women around the world will be positively impacted. We believe that, as women, we are called to fight injustice in the world. Just as God placed Eve in the garden to right a wrong, He has placed women on earth to right many wrongs. As we grow into His call on our lives, He reveals the injustice we are purposed to fight.

How We Accomplish Our Mission
We will unite, grow, and fight injustice by bringing women of faith together online and in groups in their local communities to grow intellectually, spiritually, and emotionally,

by helping them Move On, Move Up, and Move Out to discover and fulfill their God-given purpose.

What You Can Anticipate as NACWL Grows

- Online blogs and resources targeting the three areas of growth: Moving On, Moving Up, and Moving Out
- Coaching, counseling, and classes targeting the needs of women of faith as they seek God's purpose for their lives
- information to join or start your own NACWL local chapter
- Information for local workshops
- Online small-group Bible studies that focus on the topic of women and their journey toward God's purpose
- A prayer page that unites women in prayer
- A page dedicated to raising awareness of the injustices against women in our world
- All this and so much more

Visit www.NACWL.com to learn more and join the movement.

Karen Zeigler is passionate about helping women become the leaders they're created to be, and she knows firsthand that sometimes the journey of discovery can be a long one. Raised by her grandmother in a small town in Georgia, Karen longed to break free from her impoverished circumstances and explore the world. The way out seemed to be a degree in finance, which she obtained from Florida State University before embarking on a twenty-year career in the financial industry. Over the years she grew from manager trainee, to vice president, to adviser to millionaires. But brewing under the surface was her dream to speak, write, and inspire others to discover and fulfill God's purpose for their lives.

Happily married for thirty-one years to her high school sweetheart, with whom she has a college-aged daughter. Karen is the founder of the National Association of Christian Women Leaders Inc. www.nacwl.com An organization that's goal is to inspire, encourage & facilitate personal growth and leadership in today's women of faith.

47821124R00049

Made in the USA
Charleston, SC
18 October 2015